Cleft Talk for Kids

by Melissa
Johnston-Burnham, LCSW

Illustrated by
Andrea Fountain

ISBN: 1482367831
ISBN 13: 9781482367836
Library of Congress Control Number: 2013902917
CreateSpace Independent Publishing Platform
North Charleston, South Carolina

To Tucker and Roarke,
for your understanding and acceptance.
My heart smiles every day because of you.

INTRODUCTION

When my husband and I set out to adopt our daughter in 2010, it was well-known to our sons that the sibling coming home would be different from them in three key ways: She was a girl; she was Chinese; and she had a severe cleft lip and palate. The Chinese and female aspects were easy enough for them to understand. They promptly deduced, "So she doesn't speak English, and she probably likes pink."

Her cleft lip and palate were slightly more challenging to explain. I started by showing them a picture of their new sister and, like any good parent, googled the rest of the information I needed. I then pieced it all together, translated it into kid language, and (ta-da!) gave them the grand explanation of their sister's cleft lip and palate. My oldest son, who was in second grade at the time, took his sister's picture to school the next day and without any difficulty was able to tell all his friends that his sister was born with a big hole in the roof of her mouth. Needless to say, I was very pleased with his explanation!

It wasn't until two years later that I began to check online and in stores for books on cleft lip and palate. I thought it was time for my daughter to become more familiar with her condition and begin to understand why she would continue to need a lot of surgeries and speech therapy. I found some amazing, creative stories for kids about clefts, but what I really wanted was an educational book that was interactive, informative, and easy to understand.

One Monday morning, as I sat in the waiting room at Children's Hospital Colorado, I started writing. Four hours later, my daughter had completed her ninth procedure under general anesthesia, and I was done with a pretty good first draft of what would become *Cleft Talk for Kids*. I have no formal training as a writer and certainly have never attended medical school. But I am a mom who is also lucky enough to work professionally with children. As a result, I am continuously being taught what kids need and the kinds of things they appreciate. I hope *Cleft Talk for Kids* meets these expectations for any young reader and their caregivers.

AUTHOR'S NOTE

Because of the numerous types of cleft lip and palate that can occur, I chose to focus primarily on two types in this book so the concept is less confusing and tedious for young readers. However, whenever the term "cleft" is used in this book, I am referring to cleft lips, cleft palates, and all the variations of both.

Hi! My name is Kate, and this is my best friend, Charlie. If you are reading this book, then you probably know someone with a cleft lip and palate. Maybe you have a cleft. Maybe it's a friend or a family member. Maybe it's someone you don't know but have seen before, and you are curious because they look or sound different to you. You may have even thought to yourself or said to them, "What's wrong with your lip?"

Both Kate and I have a cleft lip and palate, so we thought we could tell you about them. Then you will understand a little better why a person with a cleft lip and palate looks and sounds the way they do and feel more comfortable when you see them. Are you ready?

First, where are your lips? C'mon, point to them. Do you know what those things can do? Lips have many jobs and talents.

They smile.

They pucker when you eat something sour.

They let you blow "raspberries"
at your baby brother when he is bugging you.

They help you say words like "baseball" and "popcorn."

They keep bugs from getting stuck in your teeth during bike rides.

They also help you kiss someone you love, like your mom or dad, or maybe even your baby sister when she is being nice.

Now that you know some of the things your lips can do, let's talk about your palate. What is a palate, anyway? Your *palate* is also called the roof of your mouth. It helps separate your mouth from your nose. Most everyone is born with a *hard palate* and a *soft palate*. The hard palate is at the front of the roof of your mouth and is made of bone. The soft palate is at the very back of the roof of your mouth and is made of muscle. The soft palate also has a small piece of fleshy tissue that hangs off of its end called the *uvula* (You say it like this: you-view-la). You can see this hanging down if you look in a mirror, open your mouth, and say "AAAAHHHH!" like you do at the doctor's office.

Do you know what your palate does? Believe it or not, like your lips, it has many jobs and talents. It helps you make certain speech sounds like "sss" in snake and "kkk" in cake.

It helps you sing. La la la la la!!!

It makes a tunnel in your mouth
and helps food go down your throat.

It keeps your jaw in a curved shape so your teeth don't grow in the middle of your mouth.

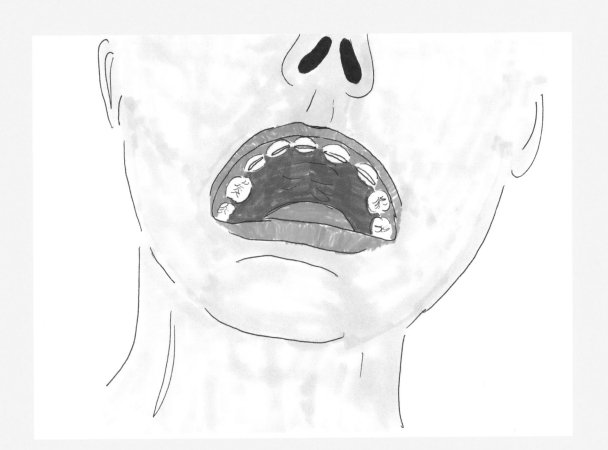

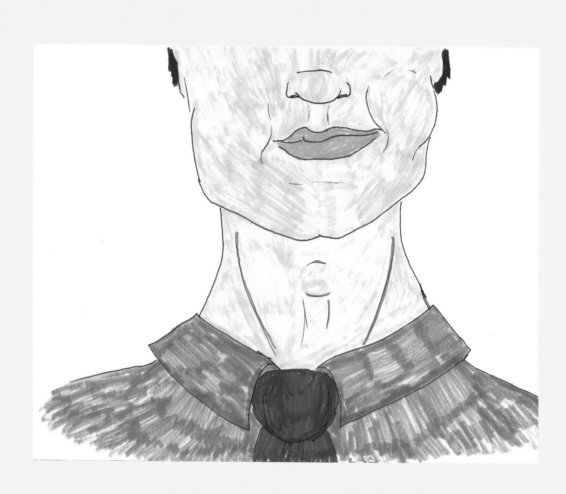

It allows you to breathe and chew food at the same time.

Just for a minute, take your tongue and put it on the roof of your mouth behind your teeth. Move your tongue all around. Do you feel all the smooth skin and how your tongue fits just perfectly up there? Guess what? If you had a cleft, you might feel a big hole you could put your tongue in, kind of like a little cave in the middle of your mouth. And with a cleft, you most likely wouldn't be able to see the uvula hanging down if you looked in the mirror.

A *cleft* is an opening or separation in something. Before you are born, you start out having clefts that close as you grow in your mother's belly. Your head actually begins as two separate pieces that join together. If the sides of your lips and palate don't come all the way together as your head develops, you will be born with a cleft lip and/or cleft palate.

There are many different kinds of clefts, but we are going to talk about the two you might notice most often. I have a *bilateral* cleft lip and palate. What other word do you know that starts with *bi*? That's right! Bicycle. *Bi* means two. So just like a bicycle has two wheels, bilateral clefts have two openings. I had two openings in my lip and two openings in my palate when I was born.

I have a *unilateral* cleft lip and palate. What other word do you know that starts with *uni*? That's right! Unicycle. *Uni* means one. So just like a unicycle has one wheel, a unilateral cleft has one opening. I had one opening in my lip and one in my palate when I was born.

Do you want to know why Kate and I were born with clefts and other people weren't? Scientists have found a lot of possible answers. The first reason is *heredity*. If a mom or a dad was born with a cleft, their child could be born with a cleft, too. You inherit it, kind of like how you get your eye color or hair color from your parents.

Clefts are also thought to happen because of things in our environment. An unborn baby can be exposed to certain medicines or harmful things called *toxins* while in their mother's belly. If an unborn baby doesn't receive enough of the good *vitamins* they need while they are developing inside their mother, a cleft might form. Most often doctors will tell you that clefts just happen by chance. In other words, nobody really knows why they happen!

Actually, clefts happen more often than you probably realize. About one in six hundred children is born with a cleft. Do you know six hundred other kids? Think about it for a minute. That may be the number of kids in your school. That means you might know at least one person with a cleft.

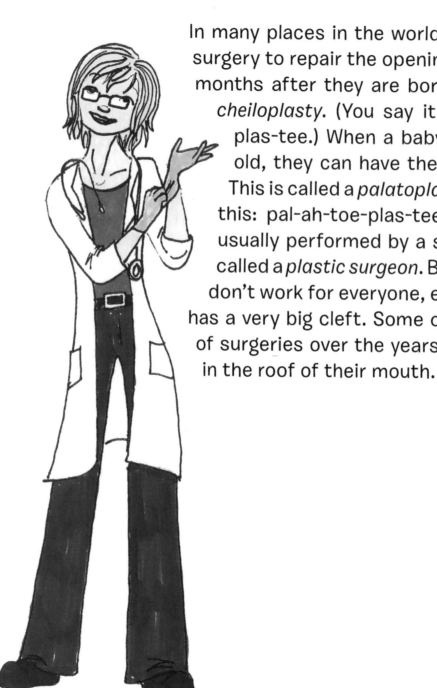

In many places in the world, a baby can have surgery to repair the opening in their lip a few months after they are born. This is called a *cheiloplasty*. (You say it like this: kigh-lo-plas-tee.) When a baby is around a year old, they can have their palate repaired. This is called a *palatoplasty*. (You say it like this: pal-ah-toe-plas-tee.) This surgery is usually performed by a specialized doctor called a *plastic surgeon*. But these surgeries don't work for everyone, especially if a baby has a very big cleft. Some children need a lot of surgeries over the years to close the hole in the roof of their mouth.

In some countries, babies can't have their lips and palates closed because their families are very poor or because there aren't any doctors available to do the surgery. So sometimes you might see kids from other countries who are older and still have lips and palates that are unrepaired. You will notice a split or two in their upper lip and probably be able to see their teeth and gums. A lot of people feel very shocked or surprised when they see this. But we promise, even though this looks different or even a bit scary, clefts do not hurt.

When a baby has a cleft, they eat from special bottles while sitting upright because they can't suck the milk from the bottle. Cleft bottles are usually plastic and squeezable so an adult can help the baby get enough food. Babies with clefts sometimes cough a lot, and they can sound like they are choking when they are drinking. They usually burp and spit up more and drool a lot, too. But don't worry. This all goes away after the cleft is closed.

There are other things that can be a problem for older kids with clefts that have not been repaired. Have you ever laughed so hard that milk came out of your nose? This can actually happen more often when kids have clefts. Food might dribble out of a baby's nose when they are eating, or they might sneeze food out of their nose after they have a snack. Bigger kids might have trouble using a straw or drinking from a drinking fountain. Some kids even have trouble doing things like blowing bubbles, whistling songs, or blowing out candles on their birthday cake.

Can you imagine how you would feel if you couldn't blow out your birthday candles or whistle your favorite song?

After a person has surgery for their cleft lip, they will have a scar or two between the bottom of their nose and the top of their mouth. The scar can be on one side like mine, or on two sides like Kate's. Their noses may also look a little flat or even bigger on one side.

Once the person is a teenager, a plastic surgeon can operate on their nose to change how it looks. This is called a *rhinoplasty*, but it has nothing to do with rhinoceroses, just noses.

When someone has a cleft, you will probably notice that they have to go to a lot of doctor's appointments. In fact, kids with clefts have a whole team of doctors who work together to provide them with special care. In addition to plastic surgeons, another important doctor for kids with clefts is an *ENT*, or an ear, nose, and throat doctor. Their fancy name is *otolaryngologist*. (You say it like this: oh-toe-lair-in-gol-oh-jest.) Like plastic surgeons, an ENT is a specialist and knows how to repair clefts and other things, too. Lots of times, children with clefts have problems with ear infections caused by fluid that builds up in their ears. This can affect their ability to hear the way they should.

Plug your ears with your fingers for a minute and try to listen to what is around you. Things sound muffled, don't they? Can you imagine if you heard like that all the time? ENTs can perform surgery to put tubes inside a child's ears to help drain the fluid. Then another specialist, called an *audiologist*, can test the child's ears to make sure they are hearing clearly like you do when your fingers aren't stuck in your ears.

Another type of specialist who helped Charlie and me for a very long time was a *speech-language pathologist*. Besides having problems eating, kids with clefts have a hard time making correct word sounds when they speak. Before we started working with our speech-language pathologists, we were a little hard to understand. Everything we said sounded like it started with M's or N's until we learned how to use our lips and palate the correct way. We both met with our speech-language pathologists every week, and after a few years of playing fun games with letters and words, we could speak much more clearly.

Children with clefts also spend a lot of time at the *dentist* and *orthodontist*, beginning when they are very little. They are more likely to get cavities, especially in their baby teeth. Brushing is extra important for them, and so is visiting the dentist regularly in case they have cavities that need to be treated.

Most children don't visit the orthodontist for the first time until they are in elementary school. An orthodontist can tell them if they need braces to straighten out their jaws and teeth. Kids with clefts often see the orthodontist when they are much younger, and braces are not the only thing they can do to help kids with clefts.

An orthodontist can also make a special type of device, called an *obturator*, which can plug up a hole in the palate (You say it like this: ob-tu-ray-tor). Most kids who wear an obturator think it looks a lot like the retainer that kids wear after they have braces except it doesn't have the front wire. But instead of keeping their teeth straight, obturators help them have an easier time eating and making speech sounds until the cleft can be closed with surgery.

The next thing that we want to talk to you about is a very hard thing for us to share. But you need to know this because we don't want to hide anything from you. Okay...here goes. In some areas of the world, children with clefts are thought to be cursed or evil just because they are born looking a little differently. They are not allowed to go to school or have a job. They rarely ever have any friends because people don't understand that a cleft is a medical condition and are afraid of how it looks. A lot of parents will even keep their kids away from playing with children who have clefts. Can you imagine how bored you would feel if you were forced to stay home all day and never had the chance to learn anything? Can you imagine how lonely you would feel if you never got to play hide and seek, go to a birthday party or play on a sports team with other kids? We know this would make us feel sad and angry, too.

Kate and I hope we have told you enough about clefts that you won't feel like you have to stay away from people who are born with them. We understand that when you first meet someone with a cleft, you might think of them only as "the kid with the cleft." But did you know that even though we have clefts that make us different from you, there are ways that we are the same, too?

My favorite food is ice cream, and I love to shop for clothes at the mall. I like to read and ride horses, and my favorite color is pink. I go to ballet class three times per week, and I danced a solo in my last recital. I also think I want to be a veterinarian when I grow up, but I'm not sure yet. My mom says I still have plenty of time to decide.

I like bacon cheeseburgers and listening to loud music. I'm a drummer in my school's band, and I play as many video games as I can without my parents getting mad. My hockey team is the second best peewee team in the state, and I play left wing. I also love to yo-yo, and my best trick is shoot the moon.

What do you like to do? What are your favorite things? Now that you know about clefts, you don't need to feel shy or afraid around a person who has one. Next time you see a kid your age who has a cleft, smile and say "Hi!" Then start talking to them like you would anyone else you meet. They might like a lot of the same things you do. You should ask them!

Before we go, we need to talk to you about one last thing. Remember how you learned earlier that clefts are something that children are born with that happen by chance? Have you ever been bullied for something that you were born with, like needing to wear glasses or being shorter than other kids your age? Have you ever been teased because you have freckles or big feet? How did this make you feel? Making fun of how someone with a cleft looks, or teasing them about any of the things they do differently hurts their feelings, too. Please remember that no matter how different a person looks or sounds, we all have the exact same feelings inside, and we all want to have friends.

And sometimes kids with clefts can make
the best friends. Right, Charlie?
The *very* best, Kate.

GLOSSARY

Palate- the roof of the mouth.

Hard palate- the front of the roof of the mouth that is made of bone.

Soft palate - the very back of the roof of the mouth that is made of muscle.

Uvula (you-view-la)- a small piece of fleshy tissue that hangs off the end of the soft palate.

Cleft- an opening or separation in something.

Bilateral- affecting two sides.

Unilateral - affecting one side.

Heredity- the passing of traits to children from their parents or ancestors.

Toxin- a poisonous substance.

Vitamins- essential nutrients the body needs in small amounts for good health and development.

Cheiloplasty (kigh-lo-plas-tee)- surgical repair of a defect in the lip.

Palatoplasty (pal-ah-toe-plas-tee)- surgical correction or reconstruction of the palate.

Plastic Surgeon- a doctor who specializes in the repair or re-formation of missing, injured, or malformed tissues or parts.

Rhinoplasty-plastic surgery of the nose.

Otolaryngologist (ENT) (oh-toe-lair-in-gol-oh-gest) - a doctor who specializes in diagnosing and treating diseases of the head and neck, especially those involving the ears, nose, and throat.

Audiologist- a professional who studies and treats hearing defects.

Speech-Language Pathologist- a professional who evaluates and treats patients with speech, language, cognitive-communication and swallowing issues.

Dentist- a professional who practices the prevention, diagnosis, and treatment of diseases, injuries, and malformations of the teeth.

Orthodontist- a specialized dentist who deals with the prevention and correction of irregular teeth, as by means of braces.

Obturator (ob-tu-ray-tor)- a device that closes or blocks an opening in the body.

www.wikipedia.org
www.thefreedictionary.com
www.merriam-webster.com

NATIONAL RESOURCES FOR PARENTS

"The Cleft Palate Foundation (CPF) is a 501(c)(3) nonprofit organization whose mission is to enhance the quality of life for individuals affected by cleft lip and palate and other craniofacial birth defects. CPF was founded by the American Cleft Palate-Craniofacial Association in 1973 to be the public service arm of the professional Association." www.cleftline.org

"The American Cleft Palate-Craniofacial Association (ACPA) is an international non-profit medical society of health care professionals who treat and/or perform research on birth defects of the head and face. The members of ACPA serve an extremely important role in the management of children and adults with cleft lip, cleft palate, and craniofacial anomalies. For over 65 years, their goal has been to provide optimal care for this group of patients and their families. Because of the diverse needs of these patients, and the required services of many different specialists, interdisciplinary cooperation and team care is essential to the patients served." www.acpa-cpf.org

"ASHA is the national professional, scientific, and credentialing association for more than 166,000 members and affiliates who are audiologists, speech-language pathologists, speech, language, and hearing scientists, audiology and speech-language pathology support personnel, and students. Their vision is making effective communication, a human right, accessible and achievable for all. Their mission is empowering and supporting audiologists, speech-language pathologists, and speech, language, and hearing scientists through: advancing science, setting standards, fostering excellence in professional practice, and advocating for members and those they serve." www.asha.org

"Shadow Buddies are condition-specific dolls designed to be a friend 'just like me' for seriously ill or medically challenged children. The Buddies not only provide comfort to the ill child, but also provide physicians a hands-on method of educating newly diagnosed children and their families about a particular disease or medical condition and its treatment. Shadow Buddies are also a unique form of play therapy. The Buddies remain with the child throughout their treatment, providing long-term psychological support. Each Buddy wears a smile on its face and has heart eyes for love. Our goal is to help these children view themselves in a positive manner." www.shadowbuddies.org

"Clefts are a major problem in developing countries where there are over one million children who are suffering with unrepaired clefts. Most cannot eat or speak properly. They aren't allowed to attend school or hold a job. These children face very difficult lives filled with shame and isolation, pain and heartache because they are viewed as outcasts and ostracized. Every child born with a cleft anywhere in the world should have the opportunity to live a full, productive life. Our mission is to provide a child born with a cleft the same opportunities in life as a child born without a cleft." www.smiletrain.org

"Operation Smile is an international children's medical charity that heals children's smiles, forever changing their lives. As an international charity for children, we measure ourselves by the joy we see on all of the faces we help. At Operation Smile, we're more than a charity. We're a mobilized force of medical professionals and caring hearts who provide safe, effective reconstructive surgery for children born with facial deformities such as cleft lip and cleft palate." www.operationsmile.org

DENVER AREA RESOURCES

www.childrenscolorado.org

www.folkplasticsurgery.com

www.foothillsspeech.org

www.rosemed.com

ACKNOWLEDGEMENTS

My utmost thanks to my daughter's plastic surgeon, Stacey Folk, MD, as well as her speech-language pathologist, Jeff Steffen, MA, CCC-SLP, for providing me with their feedback on an early draft of this book. I will be forever grateful to both of them for their talents and the extraordinary care they have provided to my daughter. It has been life changing. Cheers to Karen Wilkinson and Erika Kubat for reading the early versions of *Cleft Talk for Kids* and providing suggestions. Their kids are so lucky to have such amazing, dedicated moms. Hugs to Sarah and Zachary Winter, Angie Hamp, and Marikay White. I appreciate so much that they also took time out of their busy lives to proofread this book for me. Special thanks to Lesley Randall, Hutton's very first speech therapist. I am blessed that because she set such a lovely precedent, my daughter has never complained about having to do speech work. Thank you to the cleft team at Children's Hospital Colorado for their expertise and commitment to treating children with clefts. I can't recommend this team enough to any parent who asks where to take their child for care. High praises to Dr. Ulrich Klein at Children's Pediatric Dental Clinic for his tremendous skill and patience when my daughter screams during her orthodontic appointments. I am always very relieved to see him pull out his ear plugs! I am eternally indebted to my daughter's foster mother in China who spoon fed Hutton six times a day until she weighed enough to have her initial cleft repair. With one out of ten babies with clefts dying of starvation before their first birthday, she holds a special place in my heart. Many thanks to the youthful Andrea Fountain for her amazing illustrations. She gave this book the perfect style it needed to connect with young readers. And to Todd, Tucker, Roarke and Hutton Rose, for helping all my dreams come true.

CPSIA information can be obtained
at www.ICGtesting.com
Printed in the USA
LVHW072010170419
614533LV00012B/104/P